How
Do Simple
Machines Work?

Put
Wedges
to the Test

Sally M. Walker and Roseann Feldmann

Lerner Publications Company
Minneapolis

For Mark, Leona, Marilyn, Joyce, Jan, and Dan. Love you forever —RF

Lerner Publications Company
A division of Lerner Publishing Group, Inc.
241 First Avenue North
Minneapolis, MN 55401 U.S.A.

Website address: www.lernerbooks.com

Library of Congress Cataloging-in-Publication Data

Walker, Sally M.
    Put wedges to the test / by Sally M. Walker and Roseann Feldmann.
        p.   cm. — (Searchlight books™—How do simple machines work?)
    Includes index.
    ISBN 978–0–7613–5325–6 (lib. bdg. : alk. paper)
    1. Wedges—Juvenile literature. I. Feldmann, Roseann. II. Title.
TJ1201.W44W35 2012
621.8—dc22   46H 9026   2009032230

Manufactured in the United States of America
1 – DP – 7/15/11

Contents

Chapter 1
WORK

You do work when you plant flowers. What are other examples of doing work?

You work every day. At home, one of your chores may be planting flowers. At school, you work when you cut paper for a project.

You are working when you push a toy boat in the water. You are also working when you bite into an apple or a cookie. It may surprise you to learn that playing and eating are work too!

You do work when you eat.

Work = Using Force to Move an Object

When scientists use the word *work*, they don't mean the opposite of play. Work is using force to move an object from one place to another. Force is a push or a pull. You use force to do chores, to play, and to eat.

You use force when you lift a box.

This girl is moving a wagon from one place to another, so she is doing work.

Sometimes you push or pull an object to move it to a new place. Then you have done work. The distance that the object moves may be long or short. But the object must move.

Making PB&J Is Work!

Using a knife to remove peanut butter from a jar is work. Your force moves the peanut butter from the jar onto the knife. Then you use force to spread the peanut butter on a slice of bread.

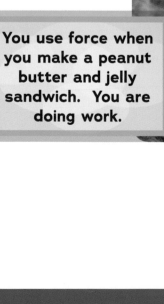

You use force when you make a peanut butter and jelly sandwich. You are doing work.

These kids are using force to push against this building. But the building is not moving. Are the kids doing work?

But Pushing a Building Isn't Work

Pushing a building is not work. It's not work even if you sweat. If you push until your arms hurt, it still is not work. No matter how much you push the building, you have not done work. Why? Because the building has not moved. If the building moves, then you have worked!

Chapter 2

MACHINES

Most people want to make work easier. Machines are tools that make work easier. Some of them make work go faster too.

A bulldozer is a machine with many moving parts. What do we call machines with many moving parts?

Complicated Machines

Some machines have many moving parts. We call them complicated machines. It may be hard to understand how complicated machines work. Steam shovels and bulldozers are complicated machines.

A steam shovel is a complicated machine.

Simple Machines

Some machines are easy to understand. They are called simple machines. Simple machines have few moving parts.

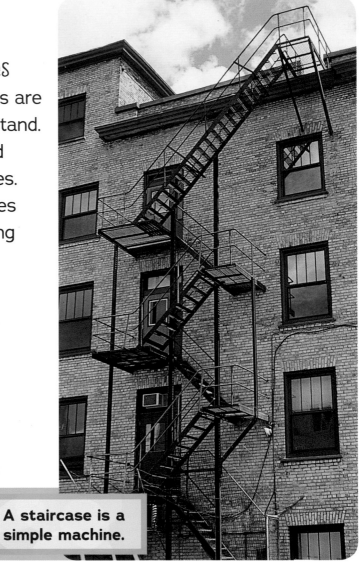

A staircase is a simple machine.

Simple machines are found in every home, school, and playground. They are so simple that you might not realize they are machines.

A doorknob has few moving parts. It is a simple machine.

Chapter 3

WHAT IS A WEDGE?

A wedge is a simple machine. At least one side of a wedge is slanted. Sometimes two sides are slanted. One end of a wedge is wider than the other end.

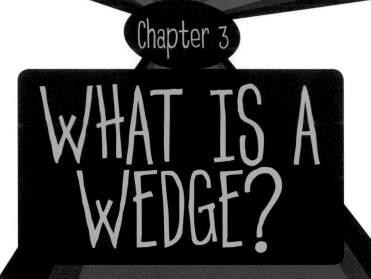

Many doorstops are wedges. What are some characteristics of a wedge?

Another kind of simple machine is also slanted. It is called an inclined plane. A ramp is an inclined plane. An inclined plane stays in place when you use it. A wedge often moves when it is used to make work easier.

This girl is using an inclined plane.

Try This!

You can prove that wedges make work easier. You will need a large sink and a cardboard rectangle that is about 10 inches (25 centimeters) long and 5 inches (13 cm) tall.

Fill the sink with water. Hold one of the 5-inch-long edges in each hand. Put the cardboard in the water at one side of the sink. The thin edge of the cardboard should touch the bottom of the sink. The wide, flat surface of the cardboard should be facing the other side of the sink. Push the cardboard through the water to the other side of the sink. Why is this hard to do?

It is hard to push the cardboard through the water.

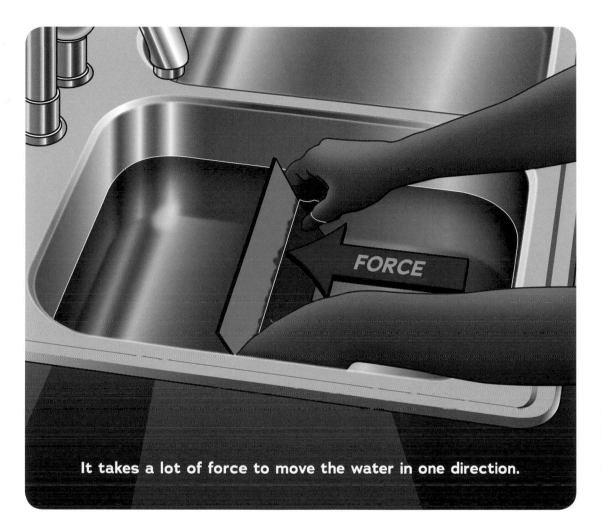

FORCE

It takes a lot of force to move the water in one direction.

It is hard because you must use a lot of force. Your pushing force moves a lot of water in one direction. And it moves all the water at the same time.

Take the cardboard out of the water. Fold it in half sideways to turn it into a wedge. It should look like the letter *V.* Put the cardboard wedge into the sink. The point of the wedge should face the other side of the sink. Push the cardboard wedge to the other side of the sink.

It is much easier to push. That's because the wedge's point separates the water.

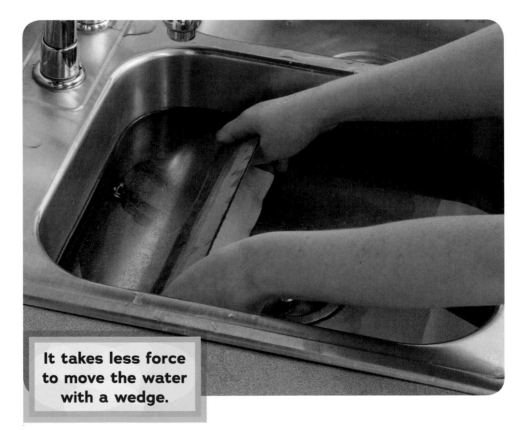

It takes less force to move the water with a wedge.

Different Kinds of Wedges

A wedge can be short and have a wide angle. Short, wide wedges can be used to split logs apart. The wedge's wide angle quickly forces the wood apart. But pounding it into the wood with a sledgehammer takes a lot of force.

SHORT, WIDE LOG-SPLITTING WEDGE

A wedge can be long and have a narrow angle. Long, thin wedges can also be used to split logs. It takes longer to split wood with a thin wedge. That's because the pushing force of a thin wedge is not as strong. But pounding it into the wood isn't as hard.

LONG, THIN LOG-SPLITTING WEDGE

How Does a Wedge Work?

Look at this person splitting a log. What direction is the hammer moving? It is moving down. This person is using a downward force.

You use a downward force when you swing a hammer.

Look at the log. The wedge made the log separate into two pieces. Each piece moved out toward the side. The wedge changed the direction of the man's downward force. The wedge changed the downward force into a sideways force. The sideways force split the log apart. If the man had tried to pull the log apart with his hands, he could not have done it. The wedge made splitting the log much easier.

Wedges change a hammer's downward force into a sideways force.

Chapter 4

HOW WE USE WEDGES

A wedge can be used in three different ways. The first way it can be used is to separate something. The pointed tip of a nail is a wedge. The nail's wedge makes doing work easier.

A nail is a wedge. What is one way we can use wedges?

Experiment Time Again!

Try this experiment, and prove it yourself. You will need a nail, two thick books, and the plastic lid from a tub of margarine. Ask an adult to help you.

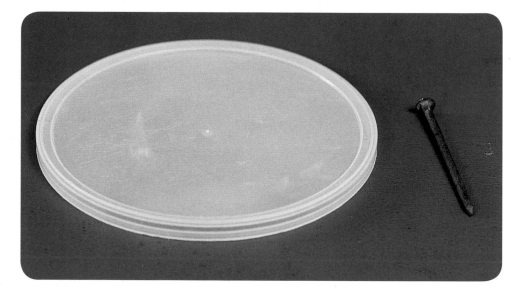

A WEDGE MAKES DOING WORK EASIER.
YOU CAN PROVE THIS FOR YOURSELF.

Place the lid on top of two books, like this. Then you won't stick yourself when you push the nail through the lid.

Push the point of the nail through the lid. Be careful not to stick your fingers. The pointed wedge on the end of the nail moves the plastic apart. The wedge makes it easier to push the nail into the lid.

Pull the nail out. Turn it around. Try to push the flat head of the nail through the lid. Can you do it? You probably can't. Pushing the flat end of the nail through the lid would be very hard work. The wedge at the tip of the nail makes the work much easier.

It would take a lot of force to push a flat object through a lid. It takes much less force to push a wedge through a lid.

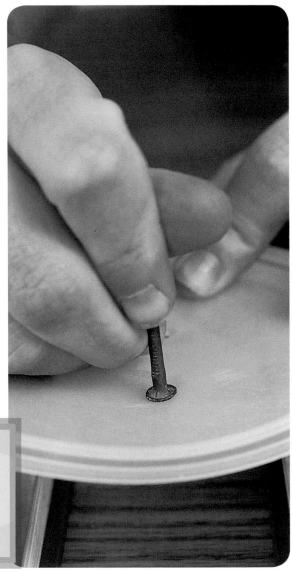

A Second Way We Use Wedges

A wedge can be used a second way. A wedge can be used to lift an object. People use a dolly to move heavy boxes. A dolly has a flat platform. Look at the front of the dolly's platform. It is a wedge. It is easy to push the wedge under the heavy boxes. That lifts them off the floor. The dolly's handle and wheels make it easy to carry the boxes to a new place.

The front of this dolly's platform is a wedge.

A Third Way We Use Wedges

A wedge can be used a third way. It can be used to hold an object in place. A wedge-shaped doorstop holds a door in place on a windy day. The doorstop slightly lifts the door. The weight of the door presses on the wedge. The wedge presses on the floor. All the pressing keeps the wedge from moving. Since the wedge stays in its place, the door can't blow shut.

A wedge-shaped doorstop holds this door open.

Everyday objects such as bark can act as wedges.

This wagon has a wedge behind its wheel. The wedge holds the wagon in place. It stops the wagon from rolling down the hill.

Chapter 5

WE USE WEDGES EVERY DAY

Wedges are all around us. We use them every day to make our work easier.

Chisels are wedges. Chisels cut into rock or wood. What is another everyday example of a wedge?

Wedges Everywhere

You use wedges at mealtimes. The tine of a fork is a wedge. A fork's tine pushes into food so you can pick it up. The blade of a knife is a wedge. It separates your sandwich into two halves.

A fork's tines are its pointed prongs. They help you pick up food.

Your front teeth are also wedges. They cut into an apple and separate a bite-sized piece from it. A shark's mouth is filled with wedges!

It would be tough to eat an apple without your front teeth.

The front of a boat is called the bow. The bow of a boat is a wedge. A wedge-shaped bow helps a boat move easily through the water.

This boat's wedge-shaped bow helps it push through the water.

The shape of a dolphin's snout helps the animal swim.

The snout of a dolphin acts like a wedge. It helps separate the water so it flows smoothly around a dolphin's body. You do the same thing when you point your hands above your head when you dive into water.

The edge of a spatula is a wedge. A spatula's wedge makes lifting pancakes easy work. It would be hard to lift pancakes with your fingers.

This cook is using a spatula to lift pancakes.

The sharp points of a staple are wedges. The two points separate the paper when you staple them into it. The ends of a staple remover are wedges too. They force the curled ends of a staple to become straight. That makes it easier to remove the staple from the paper.

Both staples and staple removers are wedges.

Wedges Make Work Easier!

Using a wedge can make your work easier. It can help you split something apart. It can help you lift an object. It can even hold an object in place. A wedge changes the direction of force. When it does, you don't have to work as hard.

Using simple machines gives you an advantage. An advantage is a better chance of finishing your work. Using a wedge is almost like having a helper. It makes your work easier. And that's a real advantage!

Using a simple machine is almost like having a helper.

Glossary

angle: the corner formed by the meeting of two lines or sides

complicated machine: a machine that has many moving parts

force: a push or a pull

inclined plane: a slanted simple machine that stays in place when used

simple machine: a machine that has few moving parts

wedge: a simple machine with at least one slanted side

work: moving an object from one place to another

Learn More about Simple Machines

Books

Christiansen, Jennifer. *Get to Know Wedges*. New York: Crabtree Publishing Company, 2009. Find out more about wedges and how we use them.

Gosman, Gillian. *Wedges in Action*. New York: PowerKids Press, 2011. See examples of wedges and how they work.

Walker, Sally M., and Roseann Feldmann. *Put Inclined Planes to the Test*. Minneapolis: Lerner Publications Company, 2012. Read all about inclined planes, another important simple machine.

Way, Steve, and Gerry Bailey. *Simple Machines*. Pleasantville, NY: Gareth Stevens, 2009. This title explores a variety of simple machines, from wheels and axles to ramps and levers.

Websites

Edheads: Simple Machine Activities
http://www.edheads.org/activities/simple-machines
Learn about simple and complicated machines as you play games and explore a house and a toolshed.

Quia—Simple Machines
http://www.quia.com/quiz/101964.html
Visit this site to find a challenging interactive quiz that allows budding physicists to test their knowledge of simple machines.

Simple Machines
http://sln.fi.edu/qa97/spotlight3/spotlight3.html
This website features brief information about simple machines and helpful links you can click on to learn more.

Index

Photo Acknowledgments

All images provided by Andy King except for the following: © Absodels/Getty Images, p. 5;
© iStockphoto.com/Tabitha Patrick, p. 7; © Monkey Business Images/Shutterstock Images,
p. 8; © Stephen Mcsweeny/Shutterstock Images, p. 10; © vnovikov/Shutterstock Images, p.
11; © iStockphoto.com/Rob Cruse, p. 14; © Todd Strand/Independent Picture Service, pp. 16, 18
© Laura Westlund/Independent Picture Service, pp. 17, 19, 20; © Tina Manley/Alamy, pp. 21, 22;
© Roman Sigaev/Shutterstock Images, p. 23; © iStockphoto.com/Johnnyscriv, p. 27; © Helene
Rogers/Art Directors & Trip/Alamy, p. 28; © Richard Williams/Alamy, p. 30; © Dave & Les Jacobs/
Blend Images/Getty Images, p. 31; © Collection 85/Glow Images/Alamy, p. 32; © Horizon/Horizon
International Images Limited/Alamy, p. 33; © James Gritz/Photodisc/Getty Images, p. 34; © Ronnie
Kaufman/Larry Hirshowitz/Blend Images/Getty Images, p. 35; © Will Croker/The Image Bank/
Getty Images, p. 36.

Front Cover: © Mark Douet/Photographer's Choice/Getty Images.

Main body text set in Adrianna Regular 14/20.
Typeface provided by Chank.

Torn at page noted 3/16